The Ages:
God's Time Periods

The Ages:
God's Time Periods

Edward Henry Clayton
(1887-1972)

BIBLE STUDENT'S PRESS™

Windber, Pennsylvania

The Ages: God's Time Periods
by Edward Henry Clayton (1887-1972)
Copyright © 2014 by Bible Student's Press

Original Printing:
   Bible Student's Notebook™, 2012

Second Printing::
   First booklet edition, 2012

Third Printing::
   First book edition, 2014

Executive Editor: André Sneidar
Layout and Design: Three-in-One Publishing

Cover design by Clyde L. Pilkington, III

ISBN-13:   978-1-62904-019-6

Published by

   Bible Student's Press™
   An imprint of *Pilkington & Sons*
   P.O. Box 265
   Windber, PA 15963

For information on *Bible Student's Press*™ releases, visit
   www.BibleStudentsPress.com

For information on other Bible study resources, visits
   www.StudyShelf.com

Printed in the United States of America.

CONTENTS

Most of us are familiar with a time table, in some form or other. At school, the daily order of study is set out in timetable form, and, in workshop and factory, hours conform to an agreed on time pattern.

Transportation concerns all issue their timetables and endeavor to provide the services they offer in accordance with the published schedules, which have all been carefully planned beforehand.

If it was otherwise – if studies or duties followed no reasonable order or method, or if public transportation services operated haphazardly at the whim of any who cared to provide those services as and when fancy dictated – the result would be chaos.

THE PURPOSE OF THE AGES

The thoughtful student of Scripture must readily conclude that God's dealings with mankind *conform to a timetable*.

God has a purpose. He has revealed it in His Word, and He is working out that purpose in accord with the counsel of His Own blessed will (Ephesians 1:11), and His counsel shall stand (Isaiah 46:10).

This purpose He has called *"The purpose of the ages"* (Ephesians 3:11). In the *Authorized (King James) Version,* it is termed *"the eternal purpose,"* but a moment's reflection will show the incorrectness of this phrase.

A purpose which is *"eternal"* can have no ful-fillment – it must forever be inconclusive; but God's purpose *absolutely and certainly* will be completed and finally realized.

However, if reference is made to the *margin* of the *Revised Version* (and to the *text* of other repu-table translations), it will be seen that the exact translation of this phrase in Ephesians (3:11) is: *"the purpose of the AGES."*

This is worthy of prayerful thought, for we are thus introduced to a "time term" which indicates that, in the gradual unfolding of His vast and predetermined plan, God is working carefully ac-cording to a timetable.

Now, if a further examination is made of this verse (Ephesians 3:11), it will be discovered that God's *"purpose of the ages"* has been *"purposed"* (literally "made") in Christ Jesus our Lord. Allow this unique and blessed *fact* to grip us and to hold our minds and hearts. It is confirmed in Hebrews 1:2, where we read,

> By Whom [*i.e.,* the Son] *also He made the ages.*

In this verse, the *Authorized Version's* transla-tion of *"worlds"* is really *"ages,"* as will be readily ascertained if, again, reference is made to the *Re-vised Version* margin and to other versions. The *Scofield Bible* margin also indicates *"ages"* as the correct word in this (and other) passages.

There is no doubt at all, of course, that in Christ, God also made the *"worlds,"* for without

Him was not anything made that was made – the truth of John 1:3 is not for one moment questioned.

In Ephesians 3:11 and Hebrews 1:2, it is pertinent to stress the fact that the *ages* were made, or formed, in Christ, for this is an additional and most significant revelation.

Goɒ has a *purpose,* and this purpose is to be unfolded and realized during a period He has chosen to term "the ages" (or "the eons"), and that purpose is *centered in Christ.*

"Age" – (Gr. *aion,* or eon)

A correct understanding of the truth of the *ages* is based on an accurate rendering and consistent use of the Greek word *aion.* This word is used in the Greek Scriptures (the New Testament) in its singular and plural forms over 100 times, and the adjective *aionios* occurs over 70 times.

We will not seek the meaning of these words from secular sources, but will endeavor to determine the true meaning from the living Word of God itself. Scripture is always its own best illustrator, and the internal evidence available for our consideration is by no means scanty.

Only by a careful examination of *all* of the occurrences of the Greek words *aion* and *aionios* can an understanding of their meaning be gained. In the course of such an enquiry, it will be found that the *Authorized Version* translates *aion* by the word *"age"* on two occasions (shown hereunder), but resorts mainly to the use of two words, *viz.:* (1) *"world"* and (2) *"ever,"* although several other terms are also employed. A few representative references are selected and quoted, in which the Greek word *aion* is used, giving the *Authorized (King James) Version* translation.

World	Matthew 13:39	*The harvest is the end of the **world**.*
	Matthew 13:40	*So shall it be in the end of this **world**.*
	Mark 10:30	*In the **world** to come, eternal life.*
	Luke 1:70	*As He spake by the mouth of His holy prophets which have been since the **world** began.*
	John 9:32	*Since the **world** began was it not heard …*
	I Corinthians 10:11	*They are written for our admonition, upon whom the ends of the **world** are come.*
	Ephesians 3: 9	*The mystery, which from the beginning of the **world** hath been hid in God …*
	Ephesians 3:21	*Throughout all ages, **world** without end.*
	II Timothy 4:10	*Demas … loved this present **world**.*

	Titus 2:12	*We should live soberly … in this present* **world.**
	Hebrews 1: 2	*By Whom also He made the* **worlds.**
	Hebrews 11: 3	*Through faith we understand that the* **worlds** *were framed by the Word of God.*
Ever	Matthew 21:19	*Let no fruit grow on thee henceforward* **for ever.**
	John 8:35	*The servant abideth not in the house* **for ever** *but the Son abideth* **for ever.**
	Philippians 4:20	*Now unto God and our Father be glory* **for ever and ever.**
	Hebrews 5: 6	*Thou art a priest* **for ever** *after the order of Melchisedec.*
	II Peter 2:17	*To whom the mist of darkness is reserved* **for ever.**
	Jude 13	*To whom is reserved the blackness of darkness* **for ever.**
	Revelation 22: 5	*They shall reign* **for ever and ever.**

Ages	Ephesians 2: 7	*That in the **ages** to come He might show the exceeding riches of His grace ...*
	Col. 1:26	*Even the mystery which hath been hid from **ages and generations**, but now is made manifest to His saints.*

If the foregoing passages are examined with the thought always in mind that the words *"world," "ever"* and *"ages"* (bold typed in each reference verse) are *all* translating the *same* Greek word (*aion*), the question will present itself:

How can the *one* Greek word (*aion*) bear the meaning *"world"* with its definite time limits, for the world has a *beginning* (John 9:32, Ephesians 3:9) and an *end* (Matthew 13:39-40), and *"ever"* which indicates endlessness?

Face the matter squarely with honesty and courage, and, once this is done, it *must* be admitted that the single Greek word (*aion*) *cannot* carry meanings which are so completely opposed to one another. Remember always that God is not the Author of confusion (I Corinthains 14:33), and He would not and does not use a term which means, in one instance, one thing and, in another, its antithesis.

Thus, there is a problem presented. Is there a solution to it? There is, and it is quite straightforward – the consistent use of a *single term* which meets the requirements of *all* of the occurrences.

Is there a word which will meet such a demand and will conform to the needs of each context? There is – it is the word *"age"* which is used in two instances cited in the foregoing list (*i.e.,* Ephesians 2:7; Colossians 1:26), and which is the word so frequently suggested in the margin of the *Revised Version* and by Dr. Scofield in his notes, and used by other translators also.

Let the reader who is anxious to know the mind of God in this vital matter of His truth follow all of the occurrences of the Greek word *aion* in a reliable concordance – it is a splendid spiritual exercise – and substitute the word *"age"* (or, simply, the transliterated word *"eon"*) throughout.

Consider every reference in its context carefully and prayerfully, and the time devoted to such a study will bring, assuredly, its own reward. The discerning student will give thought to such a verse as Matthew 13:39 which speaks of the *"end of the world"* and find that it cannot be reconciled with Ephesians 3:21 which indicates the world as being *"without end."* These two verses consistently translated, read:

| Matthew 13:39 | *Now the harvest is the* **conclusion of the eon** [or, the end of the age]. |

| Ephesians 3:21 | *To Him be glory in the ecclesia and in Christ Jesus for all the generations of the eon* [single] *of the eons* [plural] – [or age of the ages].* |
| | (In this verse, the use of the singular and plural – age and ages – is entirely obscured in the *Authorized Version*). |

There is no conflict now, for there *cannot* be contradiction in the truth of God. It is with *us* that confusion belongs (Daniel 9:8).

Or, again, when reading of the withering of the fig tree (which was in itself an act of *national significance* to Israel – Matthew 21:17-22), we learn that no fruit is to grow on the fig tree "*henceforward for ever.*" Yet, the Lord Himself, parabolically, tells us of the *future resurgence of the fig tree* when replying to His disciples' question,

What shall be the sign of Thy coming and of the end of the age? (Matthew 24:3, 32).

If the phrase in Matthew 21:19 is consistently translated, it will be at once recognized that there is no discord, but complete concord:

*Let no fruit be coming on you **for the age*** (Matthew 21:19).

Israel as a *nation, typified in the fig tree,* from then on could bear no fruit until the *end of the age,* when Israel's Lord will come and bring about His nation's rejuvenation.

There are other similar instances which could be cited where apparent conflict will be at once resolved by a consistent translation of *aion,* but the two selected passages quoted will suffice to indicate the value of *concordant* translation.

Isn't it evident, then, that *aion* is not a word used in Scripture indiscriminately of a vague, shadowy endlessness, but rather is clearly indicative of a limited (albeit lengthy) period of time – a period with a definite beginning and marked by as definite a termination?

This truth is further confirmed for us by the inspired precision with which we find the word used in the following varying phrase combinations:

1. The eon (singular) of the eon (singular): Hebrews 1:8.
2. The eon (singular) of the eons (plural): Ephesians 3:21.
3. The eons (plural) of the eons (plural): Romans 16:27, Galatians 1:5 and nineteen other references.

The spiritual significance of these distinctive combinations (all of which are carefully regarded and preserved in the *Concordant Version*) is completely lost to us in most other versions by simply and quite indiscriminately translating these phrases in terms which indicate endlessness, *e.g. "for ever and ever."*

We will consider later the import of these three remarkable phrases, but in the meantime will remark that, if the Greek word *aion* by itself is *"for ever"* (that is, without end), *why* should it be necessary to use the phrase *"for ever **and** ever"* in several instances where there is the dual occurrence of the word?

If it is *"for **ever**"* – which is undeniably endless – it is surely redundant to accord further endlessness to endlessness. It is not only redundant to do so, it is silly.

The alternative explanation, that this is scriptural idiom to express, in the original, the idea of "eternity" or "unendingness," is not at all satisfactory to the careful student of the Word of God. Holy spirit is not lacking in the ability to express itself clearly at all times.

Scripture is *God's* revelation and is expressed in words, terms and structure seven times purified, as silver, in the crucible of God (Psalm 12:6). Any variation in the use of a word or term – such as we find in the three phrases presently before us – is not without adequate and valid reason; and these fine discriminations should, at least, arrest attention and induce enquiry.

Briefly, at this point, let it be said that these three phrases refer to the last, or the last two, of the sequence of five eons (ages) which, together, constitute the *"eonian times"* (Romans 16:25 etc.), and which follow this third or present *"wicked eon"* (Galatians 1:4).

Phrase "3" is in connection with the fourth and fifth eons *together,* while phrases "1" and "2" refer to the fifth eon only – the final and most glorious of all of the five eons, which is the Day of God (II Peter 3:12).

The singular beauty and vital significance of these distinctions is hopelessly obscured from us when these phrases, pregnant with the truth of God, are, without regard, classed together by translators as varying forms all expressing but the single idea of endlessness.

The saddest feature of it all is, perhaps, that the truth – and the joy which is always inseparable from the realization and appreciation of God's truth – are lost to His saints.

The well-known words used so frequently in the Tabernacle and Temple context, *"the holy of holies"* (*cf.* Numbers 4:19), are very readily understood to mean the *most* holy of the two sacred compartments. They are not thought to be terms meaning some hazy, abstract idea of holiness.

Likewise, the phrase *"King of kings and Lord of Lords"* (Revelation 19:16) is not construed to mean some indeterminate form of monarchial autocracy, but is at once recognized as pointing to **the** King of all kings, **the** Lord of all lords.

There should, then, be no difficulty in grasping and appreciating the truth that the Eon of the eons (or Age of the ages) is that final eon, or age, fraught with the transcendent glory of the accomplishment of the Beloved and Obedient Son of God, in which the *"purpose of the eons"* will be realized (Ephesians 3:11), and not a chance combination of words, slovenly handled by translators and thought to indicate some dim, cloudy and indefinable "eternity."

"Age-Lasting" – (Gr. *aionios,* or eonian)

Up until now we have confined our consideration to the Greek NOUN *aion* and its proper English equivalent *age*, or *eon*. Perhaps we might now give some thought to the adjective form *aionios* which, as has been mentioned, occurs some 70 times.

The adjective has been translated mainly as *"eternal"* or *"everlasting"* in the *Authorized (King James) Version,* once *"for ever"* and three times *"world."* A measure of inconsistency is, therefore, apparent, and this the *Revised Version* has done little to correct, for although that version gives frequent marginal alternatives for *aion* (age) (as has already been mentioned), no such correction is suggested for the *adjective.*

The *Weymouth* version, however, makes frequent use of the phrase *"of the ages"* as a rendering of *aionios,* and the *Scofield Version* notes to the *Authorized Version* indicate *"ages"* on three occasions. Other versions translate the adjective by such phrases as *"age lasting," "age enduring"* and *"eonian."*

We learn, therefore, that the words *"everlasting"* and *"eternal"* are *not* considered by all to be the exact equivalents of the Greek word *aionios.* Nor can they be, for they imply *infinity of duration* and must, therefore, *extend backwards* into the past, as well as *project* into the future. This must be borne in mind at all times when we think of this subject – "eternity" is *not a term related to the future only.* The human mind just cannot cope with such a concept.

Many of the occurrences of *aionios* are con-
nected with *life,* and the *Authorized Version*
gives *"eternal life"* or *"everlasting life"* in these
instances. The recipients of the promised life
have *not* enjoyed it "eternally" or "everlastingly"
in the past. Life will come as the gracious gift of
God in the *future.* More will be said of this matter later.

The same observations apply in the instances
where *"punishment," "damnation," "habitations"*
and *"fire"* are qualified by the adjective *aionios.*
None of these existed eternally with that infinity
of duration which knew no beginning and can
have no end, as the word "eternal" *must* imply.
These judgments are future, and having a *beginning* they cannot be correctly termed *"eternal"*
or *"everlasting."*

In three passages in the *Authorized (King
James) Version,* the translators were forced to
abandon the use of *"eternal"* or *"everlasting"* as
the translation of the Greek adjective *aionios*
and substitute the word *"world."* The three passages are listed below; the renderings of two other versions being given along with those of the
Authorized:

Romans 16:25

KJV

> *the mystery which was kept secret since the
> world began.*

Rotherham

*sacred secret, in **age-past** times, kept silent.*

Concordant

*a secret, hushed in times **eonian**.*

II Timothy 1:9

KJV

*according to His own purpose and grace, which was given us in Christ Jesus, before the **world** began.*

Rotherham

*according to the peculiar purpose and favour — which was given us in Christ Jesus before **age-during** (or age-past) times.*

Concordant

*in accord with His own purpose and the grace which is given to us in Christ Jesus before **times eonian**.*

Titus 1:2

KJV

*In hope of eternal life, which God, that cannot lie, promised before the **world** began.*

Rotherham

*In hope of life age-abiding: which God, who cannot lie, promised before **age-during** (or age-past) times.*

Concordant

*In expectation of life eonian, which God, Who does not lie, promises before **times eonian**.*

At once the question which arose in connection with the *Authorized Version* translations of the word *aion* (age) recurs and presents itself in regard to the ADJECTIVE "*aionios*":

How can the one Greek word (*aionios*) indicate endless or infinite duration in some contexts, while in others there is a finite connotation? Why did the translators of the revered *Authorized (King James) Version* reject terms expressing endlessness and use the word "world" with its time and physical *limits* in the three instances cited above?

In each of the three instances (Romans 16:25; II Timothy 1:9; Titus 1:2) the Greek adjective *aionios* qualified the Greek noun *chromos, "times,"* and therefore, as it could not be phrased "eternal times," resort had to be made to the expedient "*world.*"

Again, it has to be stressed that God does not use a word to mean that which is contradictory in its several occurrences. The difficulty with which we are confronted is resolved simply by using a term indicative of *age-duration,* and there is none better than the simple translation "*eonian,*" which is a transliteration of the Greek term.

If these passages have been read carefully, it will not have escaped notice that, in the third of the above three references (Titus 1:2) the word *aionios* occurs *twice*. In the *Authorized Version* it is translated in the first instance "eternal," and in the second *"world."* To say the very least, such rendering cannot lay any claim to consistency and is, therefore, suspect in this very matter.

The truth of the ages requires the understanding and recognition of that fact that an *aion* (age), or that which is described as *aionios* (eonian, or age-lasting), has limited duration – it has a beginning and an end. Neither term expresses endlessness, but refers to a period of time, even though such periods may be of considerable duration.

EONIAN LIFE

Of the 71 occurrences of the adjective *aionios,* 44 of them qualify the noun *"life"* in the familiar phrases *"eternal **life"*** and *"everlasting **life."*** It will be at once protested: If *aionios* is that which is of *age-duration* only, having a beginning and an end, is the promised *life,* then, not eternal?

In this connection, it will be of interest to note that Sir Robert Anderson in his book *Human Destiny* (page 65) states:

> The solemn language of Scripture, which declares aeonian life to be the peculiar blessing of the believer, loses all its significance, unless we understand the word to describe the quality of the life, and not duration merely.

This is a most interesting observation, and one worthy of careful thought. Aeonian (eonian) *life* is that life which will obtain *during the ages* (eons), and it is that *life*, the quality and nature of that *life*, which will be enjoyed as God's gracious gift in the future two ages or eons which are to follow this present *"evil eon"* (Titus 2:12, etc.)

It may be pressed, what of the *duration* of the *life* that God has promised for faith? The "UN-endingness," or future end*less*ness of the *life* in Christ Jesus, God's gracious gift to the believer, is a blessed *fact* and vital truth, and it results from the fact that all believers shall be *"made alive"* or "vivified" in Christ in His Presence (*cf.* I Corinthians 15:23). Christ abolishes death and illuminates *life* and incorruption through the evangel and will ultimately abolish the last enemy: death (I Corinthians 15:26; II Timothy 1:10).

This glorious *life*, from its inception, will be without end, although, in the first place, it is termed *"aeonian"* or *"eonian"* life, for it will last *throughout the eons* (or ages) yet to come, but its continuance will not be limited to the eons (or ages).

This will be ensured *beyond the eons,* because we are *"vivified" in Christ* (I Corinthians 15:22-23). Eonian life, then (may we repeat and stress), is the nature and quality of life appertaining *to the eons yet future,* and is the gracious gift of God in Christ Jesus our Lord (Romans 6:23).

THE AGES (EONS, AEONS)

In the foregoing an effort has been made, very simply but earnestly, to direct attention to the value of a sound and consistent rendering of the Greek words *aion* and *aionios* and, in the course of so doing, reference has been made to the truth of the ages. Some thoughts in this connection are now offered in the hope that further interest may be stimulated and understanding gained.

An *aion* (eon, aeon, age) is a period of time and is the name given to the longest segment of time mentioned in the Scripture. That there is *more* than one eon or age is discerned from several passages in Scripture, for example:

Ephesians 2: 7	*That in the **ages** to come*
Ephesians 3:11	*According to the purpose of the **ages***
Hebrews 11: 3	*Through faith we understand that the **ages** were framed by the Word of God.*

It is the sum of these ages, their duration in totality, that form the *eonian times* (*cf.* Romans 16:25; II Timothy 1:9; Titus 1:2). This is what we know as, and generally call *time.*

The infinity of duration which *preceded,* and will *succeed,* time – to which no time-term can be applied – is referred to in Scripture in the following passages:

| I Corinthians 2:7 | *God's wisdom in a secret, which has been concealed, which God designates **before the eons** for our glory (Concordant Version).* |
| I Corinthians 15:28 | *That God may be **All in all** (Concordant Version).* |

From these Scriptures (and others) we learn that there are ages (eons) and, as there is mention of Divine activity *before* the *ages*, the *ages* or *eons* must, of necessity, have had a definite beginning.

Scripture also tells us of an *end* or *consummation* of the *ages* (eons):

I Corinthians 15:24	*Thereafter the **consummation** (Concordant Version).*
I Corinthians 10:11	*To whom the **consummations** of the eons have attained (Concordant Version).*
Hebrews 9:26	*At the **conclusion** of the eons, for the repudiation of sin through His sacrifice, is He manifest (Concordant Version).*

Although *each* age varies in its length, and the duration of time (or *eonian times*, Romans16:25 etc.) will span many millenia, the ages have a *commencement* (beginning) and they will have an *end* (comsumation, conclusion) *individually* and *collectively*.

Thus neither an age (eon) nor the *sum* of the duration of all of the ages, is the equivalent of "eternity." If we really desire a proper under-standing of the truth of God in this matter (as in others), the period of the ages (eons) – although lengthy – is *limited,* and *must never be construed* in our minds to mean that infinity of duration which is implied by, and required by, the *NON-*Scriptural terms "*eternal*" and "*eternity.*"

Before the Eons (ages)	Eonian Times (age-times)	God the Father All in all
I Corinthians 2:7	Romans 16:25	I Corinthians 15:24-28
II Timothy 1:9	II Timothy 1:9	
Titus 1:2	Titus 1:2	The Son Himself subject.

THE NUMBER OF AGES (EONS)

The mention of the truth of the *eons* will natu-rally raise in the mind the question, "*How many ages* are there in the Divine Calendar?"

As we have already seen, there is more than one. A painstaking study of the Scriptures will reveal that there are five in all. We will devote some time in presenting references to these eons (ages), commencing with those relating to the *present* or current eon (age), that in which we live.

THE PRESENT AGE

II Corinthians 4:4	*In whom the god of **this eon** blinds the apprehensions of the unbelieving so that the illumination of the evangel of the glory of Christ (CV).*
Galatians 1:4	*So that He might extricate us out of the **present wicked eon** (CV).*
Ephesians 1:21	*Up over every ... name that is named, not only in **this eon,** but also that which is impending (CV).*
I Timothy 6:17	*Those who are rich in the **current eon** be charging not to be haughty (CV).*
II Timothy 4:10	*Demas, loving the **current eon,** forsook me and went to Thessalonica (CV).*

It is this *same* present, current eon (age) which is referred to in such well-known verses as Matthew 13:39-40; Luke 16:8; and 20:34, etc., and as to the end or conclusion of which the disciples enquired of the Lord (Matthew 24:3; in the *Authorized Version,* the word *"world"* is used, but this should be age or eon, the correct rendering of *aion*).

The present eon (age) is distinguished from *all* others by reason of the cross[1] of Christ. In it –

---

1. *i.e.,* "An upright stake or pale, without any crosspiece." – A.E. Knoch (*Concordant Keyword Concordance,* page 63). For more information read The "Cross": Was Christ Nailed to a "Cross" or a "Stake"? by – Clyde L. Pilkington, Jr.

this present evil age – the rulers or chief men of *this age* crucified the Lord of Glory (I Corinthians 2:8) and cast out its Prince (John 12:31).

As the cross is at the very *center* and heart of God's purpose of the ages (eons) – for upon the cross the realization of the purpose depended – this *present* eon (age) may be considered the central of five.

Two eons preceded the *present* eon and *two* are yet to follow it, and these *two future* eons (ages) are referred to collectively as *"the eons of the eons"* in such passages as:

Romans 16:27	To the only wise God ... be glory for the **eons of the eons** (CV).
Galatians 1:5	God and Father, to Whom be glory for the **eons of the eons** (CV).
Ephesians 2:7	That, in the **oncoming eons**, He should be displaying the transcendent riches of His grace (CV).
I Timothy 1:17	Now to the King of the eons ... be honour and glory for the **eons of the eons** (CV).
II Timothy 4:18	To Whom be glory for the **eons of the eons** (CV).

Paul wrote these words from the vantage point of this *present* eon (age), looking forward to these two *"ages to come"* (Oncoming Eons) (Ephesians 2:7), which will by far transcend in excellence the three eons which by then will have gone before them.

THE AGES (EONS) TO COME

All Scripture is inspired of God (literally "God-breathed), and the inspired terms used of the eons (ages) are employed with the greatest precision. A few selected passages referring to the *combined two future eons* (ages) have just been quoted in the foregoing, but these two ages are also referred to *singly* and *individually* in the following references:

(1) *The Fourth Age (Eon)* i.e., *the eon following the present*

Matthew 12:32	*It shall not be pardoned him, neither in this eon nor in that which is **impending** (CV).*
Mark 10:30	*In the **coming eon**, life eonian (CV).*
Luke 18:30	*In the **coming eon**, life eonian (CV).*
John 10:28	*They should by no means perishing **for the eon** (CV).*
Ephesians 1:21	*Not only in this eon, but in **that which is impending** (CV).*
Hebrews 6:5	*Tasting the ideal declaration of God, besides the powerful deeds of the **impending eon** (CV).*

The inception of the fourth eon (age) is marked by the promised return of Christ to the *earth*, and its thousand years' course by the righteous and glorious reign of Christ, the subject of so much of prophetic Scripture. The Great White Throne judgment session will terminate the fourth eon.

(2) *The Fifth (and Final) Age (Eon)*

| Ephesians 3:21 | To Him be glory in the ecclesia and in Christ Jesus for all the generations of the **eon** [singular] **of the eons** [plural] (*CV*). |
| Hebrews 1: 8 | Thy throne, O God, is for the **eon** [singular] **of the eon** [singular] (*CV*). |

The *fifth age* (eon) is called the *age of the age* (the eon of the eon), or *the age of the ages* (or the eon or the eons) and it bears the fruit of Christ's righteous reign in the fourth age.

It is the only age (of all five) which will not conclude in catastrophe or judgment. In this *fifth age* there will be a new heaven and a new earth, and the tabernacle of God will be with mankind and He will tabernacle with His people (Revelation 21:1-3). This is the *Day of God* (II Peter 3:12).

The need for the child of God to give close attention to the *precise* terms of Scripture in this matter of the truth of the ages (as in *all* truths of Scripture), cannot be overstressed. The value to the saint is inestimable. In this section, we have seen a *combined* reference to the *fourth* and *fifth ages* and *individual* references to each. We should always be careful to distinguish between them – the benefit to the student will be apparent.

THE FIRST TWO AGES (EONS)

From the several passages quoted earlier, it will be realized at once that there are numerous references to the *present* (*i.e., the central*) and the two *future* eons (ages). There is no direct reference to the *first two eons, as such,* but an understanding of the *fact* of their *existence* can be gleaned from consideration of the following verses, which should be read with care:

(1) Ephesians 2:2

> *Wherein in time past, ye walked according to the **course of this world.***

The phrase *"the course of this world"* is of considerable interest, but the truth it would convey is concealed from us by the use of the word *"course"* as a rendering of the Greek word *aion* in the *Authorized Version* above quoted.

The correct rendering is, simply, *"age* [eon] *of this world,"* and reference to the *margin* of the *Revised Version* (1881) will confirm this. The *Concordant Version* and *Rotherham's Emphasised New Testament* give this phrase, respectively, as follows:

> *Eon of this world*
> *Age of the world*

When the correct rendering of the phrase is given its due weight, the truth stands revealed, *viz.,* that each *aion* (*i.e.,* eon, or age) has, and synchronizes with, its own particular *kosmos* (*i.e.,* world system).

This Ephesian verse under notice connects the *present, central eon* (age) or time segment with the world order of things obtaining *from* the deluge of Noah's time (which terminated the *second eon* as indicated below), *until* the judgments and events leading up to the return of Christ to the earth.

The *"eon of this world"* is the eon and the world in which Paul (and we) once walked in accord with the *"prince of the power of the air"* (Ephesians 2:2).

If, as is now suggested, each eon (age) has its corresponding world-system, and each world-system its particular eon (age), then the discovery in Scripture of reference to *"worlds" before* the present world in which we live, will also determine for us the existence of the *related eons* (ages) prior to the present. With this suggestion, this thought, in mind, may we consider the following verses penned by the Apostle Peter as he was *"led on by Holy Spirit"*:

(2) 2 Peter 3:5-7

> *For they want to be oblivious of this, that there were heavens of old, and an earth cohering out of water and through water, by the Word of God: through which the then world, being deluged by water, perished. Yet the heavens now, and the earth …*

Here, then is a powerful reminder of the fact
(when in these days there is such willful igno-
rance of it) that there *was* a *world* which perished
in a primal deluge. This was the *world* (the heav-
ens and the earth) created by God *"in beginning"*
and which ultimately *became "chaos and vacant"*
as a result of a deluge, which was an *earlier* inun-
dation than that of Noah's days (*cf.* Genesis 1:1-2;
Isaiah 45:18).

This *world* is distinguished by Peter by the
significant phrase *"the **then** world"* or the *"the
world that then was,"* and the very *first* eon (age)
would correspond with that *first world* and run
concurrently with it.

(3) II Peter 2:5

> *And spares not the **ancient world**, but
> guards Noah, an eight, a herald of righ-
> teousness, bringing a deluge on the **world**
> of the irreverent.*

The first chapter of Genesis from the second
part of verse 2 is the inspired account of the reha-
bilitation, or restoration, from the chaos which
had resulted from a primeval cataclysm, which is
referred to in later Scriptures as *"the disruption"*
(*e.g.* John 17:24; Ephesians 1:4; I Peter 1:20; etc. –
Concordant Version).

The verse from II Peter (2:5), quoted from the
Concordant Version immediately above, relates
to that world-system which Peter terms the *"ancient"* or *"old"* world, which was the world-order

existing from the *restoration of the **first** world until the world-wide flood of Noah's time* which swept degenerate humanity from the earth, on which it had corrupted its way.

This flood (of Noah's time) is not to be confused with the deluge to which Peter refers (II 3:6). These two passages from Second Peter should be carefully studied and distinguished.

This "ancient" or "old" *world* is, then, the *second* world, or world-system. In the light of the truth derived from Ephesians 2:2, this *world* would have its related *eon* (age) – the *second eon* – occurring simultaneously with it.

In all of God's works there is law, order and arrangement, and it is in accord with the faultlessness which characterizes His designs to find in the *order* of the eons the beauty and harmony of perfect symmetry.

The central of the five eons (unique by reason of the fact that, during its course, Christ took upon Himself the form of a slave, came to be in the likeness of humanity – Philippians 2:7-8 – and endured the cross – Hebrews 12:2) is bounded by *two preceding* and *two succeeding eons.*

The complete *structure of the eons* – with the *cross* at the very heart and center and God's purpose running its destined course throughout – is thus seen to be in perfect equipoise. The structure may be indicated very simply as follows:

IN BEGINNING (Genesis 1:1)
1st EON
DISRUPTION (Genesis 1:2, etc.)
2nd EON
DELUGE (NOAH) (Genesis 6-8)
3rd EON
(Present. The Cross.)
DAY of WRATH (Revelation 6:16-17)
4th EON
(Coming or future eon.)
GREAT WHITE THRONE (Revelation 20:11)
5th EON
(Eon of eons.)
CONSUMMATION (I Cor.15:24, etc.)
GOD ALL IN ALL (I Corinthians15:28)

THE PURPOSE OF THE AGES (EONS)

The references which have already been given in relating to the five eons (ages) by no means exhaust the passages concerning them, but sufficient have been cited to bring into prominence the truth of the ages (eons), a very vital truth which has been, for too long, neglected or disregarded by many who love the Lord. It is the *privilege,* as well as the *duty,* of each child of God to become acquainted with the truth of God.

> *Thy Words were found, and I did eat them: and Thy Word was unto me the joy and rejoicing of mine heart* (Jeremiah 15:16).

We are nourished and rejoice in the measure we partake of the living Word. *All* of God's Word brings joy to the heart and not the least the truth of the ages (eons) and their related *purpose.*

The glorious theme or doctrine of the truth of the ages has, of course, as will be readily appreciated, a direct and powerful bearing on matters pertaining to *"judgment," "punishment"* and *"human destiny."*

It is beyond the scope of this present work to deal with these subjects which are, in themselves, extensive. Suffice it here to say that such matters, viewed in the glorious light of the truth of the ages are seen in sharp focus and correct perspective.

The God dishonoring dogma of *"eternal punishment"* (Matthew 25:46) and its associated belief *"tormented for ever and ever"* (Revelation 20:10, etc.) are tenets foreign to Scripture, and which the *consistent* and *concordant* translation of *aion* (eon) and *aionios (eonian)* must force us to discard.

*Un*ending punishment, never ending torment, apart from being *foreign* to the *very nature of God Who is love and light* (I John 1:5; 4:8, 16), would rob God of His ability to consummate His purpose. That could *never be.*

Throughout the ages (eons), saturated as they are (and will yet be) by the varied events which combine to form what man is pleased to term "human history," *"the purpose of the ages"* – which God makes in Christ Jesus our Lord (Ephesians 3:11) – has moved and will continue to move undeviatingly towards its complete and satisfactory fulfillment. In spite of so much that is apparently to the contrary, the working out of that purpose is in strict and irresistible accord with *"the counsel of His Own will"* (Ephesians 1:11).

No power, nor any combination of powers, can thwart the reaching of the *goal* God has in view or the ultimate realization of *His intention* (Romans 9:19).

What is that *goal?* Has God confined to us, His saints, the *ultimate* He has in mind and towards which His *purpose* is directed? He has. He did so through His inspired penman, Paul, the beloved Apostle to the Nations.

> *In all wisdom and prudence making known to us the **secret of His will** (in accord with His delight, which He purposed in Him) to have: an administration of the complement of the eras, to **head up all in the Christ** – both that in the heavens and that on the earth* (Ephesians 1:9-10, CV).

In these sublime words, *God* has declared to us *His intention: to head up all in the Christ.* Through *Christ* God made the ages (Hebrews 1:2); in *Christ* God formulated the *purpose* of the ages (Ephesians 3:11); in *Christ* God is going to *head up the all,* for, at the conclusion of the ages, **all** will be subject to the Son of God (I Corinthians 15:25-27). When that is accomplished, as assuredly it will be, then the *Son Himself* will *also* *subject* Himself to His God and Father, that *God* may be *All in all* (I Corinthians 15:28). Not part in all, or all in part, but *All in all.*

God's purpose, formulated in Christ before the ages, *required the ages* for its unfolding and realization. The concept of the ages required a correlating reason, and that reason, adequate and satisfying, was the *purpose of God,* which had its source in the *will* and *love* of *God.* The *ages* and the *purpose* required *God's Son* – He did not fail His God and Father.

> *To our God and Father be glory for the **Eons of the Eons.***
>   ~ Philippians 4:20

E.H. Clayton of Sheffield England was a great scholar of the Greek and Hebrew languages. His close association with A.E. Knoch dated from the very earliest days of the Concordant Publishing Concern.

Clayton did substantial work in the long and involved process of compiling the *Concordant Greek Scriptures*. He then spent half his life working fulltime on the *Concordant Hebrew Scriptures*. He was the author of many articles that were printed in *Unsearchable Riches* and *Grace and Truth* magazines.

Your Part

Now that you have read this book, it's your turn.

If the truths presented here have helped you, don't let these truths die in your hands.

Please write to us and let us know your thoughts concerning its content.

Consider assisting us in getting this book into the hands of those who would be encouraged and strengthened by its message:

- Recommend it to your friends and loved ones.

- Order additional copies to give as gifts.

- Keep extra copies on hand to loan to others.

If you have not read the author's other works, order them today.

We would be honored to have your fellowship in getting this book freely to those who hunger spiritually. We have daily opportunities to send it to pastors, Sunday school teachers, Bible college professors and students, Bible class teachers, and prisoners.

Enjoy Books?

Visit us at:

www.StudyShelf.com

Over the years we have often been asked to recommend books. The requests come from believers who longed for material with substance. Study Shelf™ is a collection of books which are, in our opinion, the very best in print. Many of these books are "unknown" to the members of the Body of Christ at large, and most are not available at your local "Christian" bookstore.

You Can:

Read

A wealth of articles from past issues of the *Bible Student's Notebook* ™

Purchase

Rare and hard to find books, booklets, leaflets, Bibles, etc. in our 24/7 online store.

DAILY EMAIL GOODIES™

Do you receive our
Daily Email Goodies™?

These are free daily emails that contain short quotes, articles, and studies on Biblical themes.

These are the original writings of Clyde L. Pilkington, Jr, as well as gleanings from other authors.

<u>Here is what our readers are saying</u>:

"Profound! Comforting! Calming! Wonderful!" – NC

"The Daily Email Goodies continue to bless my heart! ... They provide plenty of food for thought." – IL

"I really appreciate the Goodies!" – VA

"Your Daily Email Goodies are making me aware of authors whose names I don't even know." – GA

"I am glad to be getting the Daily Email Goodies – keep 'em coming." – IN

Request to be added to our free
Daily Email Goodies™

If you would like to be added to the mailing list, email us at:
Goodies@StudyShelf.com